PRAYING WITH POWER

PRAYING WITH POWER

*A guide for Gen Z
and everyone on how
to pray effectively
and see God's results*

GLORY TANG

Praying With Power

A guide for Gen Z and everyone on how to pray effectively and see God's results

Cover design by Joseph & Glory Tang

Published by Glory Tang

I am grateful to God for the opportunity to co-author this book with the Holy Spirit. I also want to thank my family for believing in me and supporting my commitment to Jesus. I truly appreciate and love each one of you.

This book is dedicated to young people living in one of the most critical times in human history. I believe you have a massive part in the end-time harvest, and the Kingdom of God greatly needs you to impact your generation.

No matter how young you are, God can use you for His purpose. As the apostle Paul advised Timothy, "Don't let anyone look down on you because you are young, but set an example for the believers in speech, in conduct, in love, in faith and in purity" (1 Timothy 4:12 NIV).

I encourage you, young people, to pave the way for many to the Kingdom of God by living a Christ-like life and praying fervently. Your prayers are powerful and can change people's lives and shape history.

Contents

Introduction

Prayers can become a great adventure of faith if we learn how to partner with the Holy Spirit to see prayers answered with God's astounding results. We are introduced to prayer from day one of our born-again Christian experience. We were told to pray and taught to pray as well. We know that praying is essential, but we struggle to do it consistently. At best, we say our prayers before meals and sleep, but we do not see many results and changes to crises and life's struggles. Our prayers are relegated to a dull, ritualistic routine. Discouragement starts to set in when our prayers go unanswered, and we even doubt their value. We may not want to admit it, but regrettably, all these seem so true.

I remember that as a teenager, I would feel compelled to pray, but I ran out of the "right" words to say to God. Somehow, I thought God probably might respond better if I had the right words and perfected my English. That frustrated me because I would feel profoundly intense but had no words to express them.

Then, one day, while alone in the house, I suddenly raised my voice and shouted at God. I demanded that He should respond to me and not ignore me anymore. It was hilarious as I recalled how I faced that blank wall and ranted at His non-responsiveness to my prayers. I was desperate to know He had heard and would speak to me audibly. After many years, I understood that prayer holds a deeper meaning beyond mere words and a to-do list for God. Prayer is a dialogue rather than a monologue. It is a 2-way communication in which God wants us to know His heart and responses to our feelings and requests. And He communicates with us in a myriad of ways.

Over time, I have learned that God is not so concerned with my words as my heart. He speaks in universal languages, and my language never hinders what He can do for me through my prayers. I have also discovered that prayer can be very effective when we pray according to God's will. Many do not pray effective prayers or see results because they do not understand God's will. Instead of God's will, we pray according to our selfish desires. No wonder our prayers seem to go unanswered no matter how hard we may pray. Other times, we find ourselves begging God to answer us because we are uncertain if He will hear. This starkly contrasts with our understanding from 1 John 5:14 that God listens to our prayers when we ask for things that align with His will.

As we delve into the book, I hope it brings greater understanding and reignites your passion for prayer. May you experience the joy of witnessing God's plan come to fruition on earth, surpassing even your wildest imagination through the power of effective prayer.

I

Prayer is Your Most Powerful Weapon

One day, unexpectedly, God asked me if I would ever go to war without armor and weapons. Well, of course, my answer is a definite no. It is unimaginable for anyone to go to war in civilian clothes and bare hands and expect to survive. I realized that God was emphasizing the importance of prayer in the face of spiritual warfare.

As Christians, we face spiritual battles on a daily basis. In the physical world, we know that we must adorn the proper attire and arm ourselves with the right weapons to go to war. The same principle applies in the spiritual realm. Our lack of knowledge or busy lifestyles does not excuse us from the ongoing struggle against the forces of darkness. It is crucial to recognize the existence of the demonic realm and its ongoing influence in our world today. This does not mean we must be paranoid or fearful all day. The Bible tells us to stay alert. We need to be equipped with an understanding of how to face the daily battle with God's help and power. We want to remain in victory; the good news is that God already has a strategy for us to attain that.

Let us look at Ephesians 6:10-18 NASB: "Finally, be strong in the Lord and in the strength of His might. Put on the full armor of God, so that you will be able to stand firm against the schemes of the devil. For our struggle is not against flesh and blood, but against the rulers, against the powers, against the world forces of this darkness, against the spiritual forces of wickedness in the heavenly places. Therefore, take up the full armor of God, so that you will be able to resist on the evil day, and having done everything, to stand firm. Stand firm therefore, having belted your waist with truth, and having put on the breastplate of righteousness, and having strapped on your feet the preparation of the gospel of peace; in addition to all, taking up the shield of faith with which you will be able to extinguish all the flaming arrows of the evil one. And take the helmet of salvation and the sword of the Spirit, which is the Word of God. With every prayer and request, pray at all times in the Spirit, and with this in view, be alert with all perseverance and every request for all the saints."

The apostle Paul explained how we can be strong in the Lord and the power of God's might. Firstly, know that God wants you to be strong and powerful, not in your strength but in God's. As believers, resilience and strength are defining traits of our identity. The key is to put on the full armor of God so that you can stand against the schemes of the devil, as mentioned in verse 11. Some of us may have gone through the familiar Sunday school lesson about the different components of the armor of God, but do we actively apply the truths and put them into practice?

Spiritual warfare is real. It is important to acknowledge the reality of spiritual warfare and the challenges we face every day. According to verse 12, our battle is not against other people but against rulers, powers, and the spiritual forces of wickedness in the heavenly places. This means that we may be fighting against high-ranking forces in the unseen realms of darkness. To combat this, it is critical to utilize prayer daily because it is the most effective weapon in the arsenal of Heaven.

1 Peter 5:8 tells us that the enemy prowls like a roaring lion, seeking someone to devour. "The Devil is poised to pounce and would like nothing better than to catch you napping," as the Message Bible says. The enemy is no innocent pussy cat but an evil entity fiercely hungry and looking for someone to devour. We must determine in our hearts, first and foremost, that we will not be easy prey at all.

The Battle Belongs to the Lord

The fact is, we are fighting from a secure place of eternal victory. Jesus has defeated the enemy forever on the cross and ever lives to intercede for us today. He came to destroy the devil's works.[1] We do not fight for victory but from victory henceforth.

I remember the day the Lord told me I was winning the spiritual battle as long as I stayed in the fight. That surprised me because it did not look and feel that way to me at all. The

Lord reminded me that the victory was already won at the cross. The enemy would love for us to call it quits when the battle (whatever your situation) fiercely rages against us.

The prophet Elisha had to ask God to open his servant's eyes to see the heavenly reinforcement of horses and chariots of fire surrounding them in the face of the Aramean armies.[2] When our spiritual eyes are open, we possess the proper perspective and understand that "there are more on our side than on their side."[3] Remember, God is on your side! He did not leave you alone to fight a losing battle. Every day, you are winning. Yes, you are. You must stand your ground firmly, although the enemy may attempt to test your footing, shake you, and even taunt you. Do not let the voice of Goliath intimidate you. Stand your ground and know that the battle belongs to the Lord. He never loses a battle, for sure. My friend, you cannot fail because Jesus already won.

Remember how the shepherd boy David audaciously retorted at the Philistine giant in 1 Samuel 17:45-47? "You come to me with a sword, a spear, and a saber, but I come to you in the name of the Lord of armies, the God of the armies of Israel, whom you have defied. This day the Lord will hand you over to me, and I will strike you and remove your head from you. Then I will give the dead bodies of the army of the Philistines this day to the birds of the sky and the wild animals of the earth so that all the earth may know that there is a God in Israel and that this entire assembly may know that the Lord does not save by sword or by spear; for the battle is the Lord's, and He will hand you over to us!"

Little David knew something the rest of the Israelites and Philistines were ignorant of – the battle is the Lord's. Anyone would know that if God is your opponent, there is zero chance of you winning. The little unimpressive stone in the hand of David became a powerful weapon against Goliath. That day, a record-breaking victory in Israel's military battlefield was set and recorded because David understood that the battle was God's.

Possessing a Victor's Mindset

I was talking to a young teen one day, and he was sharing his frustrations with some personal struggles. He looked dejected and downcast. In his own words, it looked like no matter how hard he tried, he would still fall into temptations, and nothing worked for him. As I listened patiently, I explained to him the importance of cultivating a victor's mindset based on God's Word. Only the truth of His Word can liberate us from the lies of the accuser of the saints. And the truth is that this teenager is a champion in Christ. In fact, all of us are champions, not losers.

The problem is that many of us try to fight spiritual battles with a victimized mindset. This mindset sets us up for failure and defeat. We imagine ourselves pitting against a huge unseen opponent, and we would always lose. The ungodly belief leads us to fall prey time and time again into temptations due to a victim's mentality. Sadly, it is almost like an effort of self-sabotage.

Listen, if you are abiding in Jesus, you are already an overcomer because He has defeated the devil once and for all. "And having disarmed the powers and authorities, He made a public spectacle of them, triumphing over them by the cross" (Colossians 2:15 NIV).

The Bible tells us that there is a direct connection between who you are and what you think. Proverbs 23:7 states, "For as he thinks in his heart, so is he." Therefore, we should not allow our daily thoughts to go unchecked because they shape us. Take a moment to reflect on whether you focus your thoughts on the positive or negative each day. Do you constantly think and dwell on the best or the worst, the good or the bad? Our minds need to be renewed and shaped by God's truth. Some of us may need to change our belief system. Have you ever spoken to someone whose conversation always leans toward negativity? Or a person who constantly expresses toxic emotions towards you? You will realize that perception of oneself and situations matters. It will affect what you say, and do and how you make decisions and live your life.

Therefore, it is pivotal for us to renew our minds according to what God says.[4] To possess a victor's mindset, we must guard over our preoccupied thoughts and emotions. With our best efforts, make it a daily practice to submit all our thoughts in obedience to Jesus.[5]

My friend, God sees you as a champion - a mighty man or woman of valor. You are the head, not the tail; above and not beneath. The Bible contains numerous promises that remind us of our victory in Christ, such as the ones I have listed below:

- *The Lord will fight for you; you need only to be still. (Exodus*

14:14 NIV)

- *The Lord will cause your enemies who rise against you to be defeated before you. They shall come out against you one way and flee before you seven ways. (Deuteronomy 28:7 ESV)*

- *This is My command—be strong and courageous! Do not be afraid or discouraged. For the LORD your God is with you wherever you go. (Joshua 1:9 NLT)*

- *"Do not be afraid of them," the LORD said to Joshua, "for I have given you victory over them. Not a single one of them will be able to stand up to you." (Joshua 10:8 NLT)*

- *No weapon that is fashioned against you shall succeed, and you shall refute every tongue that rises against you in judgment. This is the heritage of the servants of the Lord and their vindication from Me, declares the Lord. (Isaiah 54:17 ESV)*

- *When the enemy comes in like a flood, the Spirit of the Lord will lift up a standard against him. (Isaiah 59:19b NKJV)*

- *The one who breaks through goes up before them; they break through, pass through the gate, and go out by it. So their king passes on before them, and the Lord at their head. (Micah 2:13 NASB)*

- *Therefore if the Son makes you free, you shall be free indeed.*

(John 8:36 NKJV)

- *I have told you these things, so that in Me you may have peace. In this world you will have trouble. But take heart! I have overcome the world. (John 16:33 NIV)*

- *For the law of the Spirit of life in Christ Jesus has made me free from the law of sin and death. (Romans 8:2 NKJV)*

- *What then shall we say to these things? If God is for us, who can be against us? (Romans 8:31 NKJV)*

- *No, in all these things we are more than conquerors through Him who loved us. For I am convinced that neither death nor life, neither angels nor demons, neither the present nor the future, nor any powers, neither height nor depth, nor anything else in all creation, will be able to separate us from the love of God that is in Christ Jesus our LORD. (Romans 8:37-39 NIV)*

- *No, despite all these things, overwhelming victory is ours through Christ, who loved us. (Romans 8:37 NLT)*

- *No temptation has overtaken you except what is common to mankind. And God is faithful; He will not let you be tempted beyond what you can bear. But when you are tempted, He will also provide a way out so that you can endure it. (1 Corinthians 10:13 NIV)*

- *But thank God! He gives us victory over sin and death*

through our LORD Jesus Christ. (1 Corinthians 15:57 NLT)

- *But you belong to God, my dear children. You have already won a victory over those people, because the Spirit who lives in you is greater than the spirit who lives in the world. (1 John 4:4 NLT)*

- *For whatever is born of God overcomes the world. And this is the victory that has overcome the world - our faith. (1 John 5:4 NKJV)*

Use Faith!

Back to Ephesians 6:16, the English Standard Version puts it this way: "In all circumstances take up the shield of faith, with which you can extinguish all the flaming darts of the evil one."

During ancient Roman times, a soldier's shield was considered a vital tool in protecting against enemy attacks such as swords, flaming arrows, and spears. Fiery arrows were a commonly used tactic in battles.[6] In this passage, Paul uses the analogy of a shield to represent our most robust defense - our faith in God. Why? This is because the devil often attacks and influences our minds through lies and defeated, tormenting thoughts. This can lead to fear and doubt in God's love and promises.

Roman soldiers also commonly formed a battle formation by interlocking their shields to protect and advance against enemy troops.[7] This emphasizes the importance of engaging in corporate prayers with faith-filled believers during times of need and against the enemy's attacks. The power of agreement in prayer and unified faith is deadly to the forces of darkness.[8] During a crisis, it is crucial to surround yourself with believers who will pray on your behalf through spiritual intercession and believe God for your breakthrough.

Having faith is crucial for achieving breakthroughs, both for yourself and others. You may have heard the saying, "Faith is the currency of Heaven." This means that nothing happens until you exercise your faith. The transactions of Heaven operate entirely by faith. So, what does having faith in prayer mean? It means declaring what God says about your situation and adopting His perspective. Choose to believe in God's Word despite your circumstances.

Faith is vital to receiving God's outcome. What seems impossible to us can become possible through faith in Him. God responds to our faith, not our angry musings, complaints, or rationalization. The Bible records instances where Jesus credited an individual's faith for their healing. He would say to the sick – "Your faith has healed you," or "Your faith has made you well."[9] In simple terms, faith is being confident of the things we hope for and knowing that something is real even if we cannot see it. It is similar to using an ATM card and trusting that the cash will be dispensed. Just as we need to use our cards to access our bank accounts, we must use faith to access the treasuries of Heaven for the blessings and miracles we desire.

Faith is the act of holding onto something that is divinely guaranteed. By expressing your faith in prayer and declaring God's promises under challenging situations, you can experience unfathomable breakthroughs. Supernatural financial gain, successful business deals, the restoration of relationships, physical and emotional healing, phenomenal miracles, creative ideas and inventions, divine connections, and new opportunities, to name a few, will start to happen for you!

---

1 1 John 3:8
2 2 Kings 6:17
3 2 Kings 6:16
4 Romans 12:2; Philippians 4:8
5 2 Corinthians 10:5
6 bibleref.com/Ephesians/6/Ephesians-6-16.html
7 primaryhomeworkhelp.co.uk/romans/formation.html
8 Mathew 18:19
9 Mathew 9:22; Luke 17:19; 18:42

2

Understand Your Authority in Christ

The Britannica dictionary defines "authority" as the power or legal permission to do something, give orders, make decisions, or control someone or something. Jesus says that He has given us the authority to trample on serpents and scorpions, and over all the power of the enemy, and nothing shall by any means hurt you (Luke 10:19 NKJV). Notice here that Jesus has delegated to us His authority over all the enemy's power - not just some of it. All means all. So, listen again - You have authority over all the enemy's power. Wow, what a promise!

Use Your Spiritual Authority

To have spiritual authority means to have dominion, power, and rule. Authority is only effective when you use it. Spiritual authority is not mere intellectual knowledge or philosophy but the rights given by Jesus Himself to be used by all believers. It is not based on one's spiritual maturity or a special entitlement for the elites and church leaders. It is accessible to everyone in the Kingdom who has a genuine relationship with Jesus.[1]

In Mark 4:35-41 NKJV, Jesus demonstrated what authority looks like when His disciples faced a terrifying storm on the sea. In verse 39, "Then He arose and rebuked the wind, and said to the sea, "Peace, be still!" And the wind ceased, and there was a great calm." Notice the contrast between Jesus' and His disciples' reactions in this passage. Contrary to the visibly shaken disciples, Jesus knew His God-given authority and immediately commanded the winds and sea to be still. According to the Strong's concordance, the Greek word for "peace" that Jesus used is Siope - meaning to be silent, dumb, and hold peace. He also said, "Be still." In Greek, it means to muzzle and become speechless. As a result, the storm turned into an instant perfect calm.

Jesus also tells us hyperbolically that it shall be done if we speak to the mountains and command them to be removed without a doubt. "For assuredly, I say to you, whoever says to this mountain, 'Be removed and be cast into the sea,' and does not doubt in his heart, but believes that those things he says will be done, he will have whatever he says" (Mark 11:23 NKJV). This is what mountain-moving faith looks like!

It is not enough to know that Jesus has given you authority; you need to use it. Exercise your God-given authority today by commanding the storms of life, the chaos, the destructive winds, the seemingly impossible situation, the overwhelming thoughts, and the immovable mountains of hindrances to be removed, muzzled, silent, and speechless in Jesus' name! You have been authorized to do it - not in your authority but in God's.

Power is in Your Mouth

It is awe-inspiring to contemplate the power of God's Word as we read through the creation story in the Bible. In Genesis 1, the phrase "And God said" is repeated several times during the creation process. When God speaks and commands, He brings forth all creation. It is truly remarkable to think that the power of His Word has framed the entire universe.

It is, therefore, crucial to understand the potency of speaking God's Word over our lives and circumstances. When we speak His Word out loud, it has creative power and can help us overcome various challenges, such as demonic oppression, financial struggles, or health issues. We are given the spiritual authority to annihilate every demonic attack against us by declaring God's truth.

Some years ago, while caring for my little son, who had contracted hand, foot, and mouth disease, I also contracted the same infectious disease. While the symptoms were mild for my child, they were more severe for me. Besides feeling unwell and weak, I had painful blister-like sores on my hands and feet. It became unbearable when I began to feel stinging pain on the soles of my feet as I walked. I felt miserable for days until I finally decided to brace myself and spend time praying. I do not know how long I had been praying, but I felt something tangible lifted off my body at one point, and an instant shift occurred. The pain left me miraculously, and my strength was restored quickly. The breakthrough happened when I used my God-given authority to pray and declare His promises over my body and health. I was genuinely thankful for the healing and God's intervention.

My friend, you are cherished and esteemed deeply by God. He will safeguard and defend you and your loved ones. You need not confront crises or battles alone. To withstand spiritual warfare, you can declare the living Word because what you say about your situation matters. Regrettably, some of us have unwittingly empowered the enemy through careless words. For example, phrases like "I am always stepping on people's toes," "I feel rotten," "I am not good at handling relationships," "I am losing my mind," "I will never get rich," "This thing is driving me crazy!" and "My world is falling apart!" should be avoided.

Being mindful of our words and how we speak is of utmost importance. As the Bible mentions, "Death and life are in the power of the tongue, and those who love it will eat its fruit" (Proverbs 18:21 NASB). Our words can either heal or hurt others, and it is evident that a single word from God has more power than a thousand idle words. Hence, choosing our words wisely and speaking God's Word over difficult circumstances and people is crucial.

To accomplish that, it is important to establish our faith firmly in the teachings of God's Word. Reflecting on biblical principles can be incredibly helpful in navigating life's challenges and aligning ourselves with God's truths. It is essential to ask ourselves questions such as, "What does the Bible say about my fears?" or "How does God guide us through financial difficulties, negative thoughts, and feelings of rejection or shame?" By focusing on scriptural truths, we can overcome negative emotions, external pressures, and opinions of others while remaining grounded in our faith and allowing God's Word to shape our reality.

Pray According to God's Will

"This is the confidence we have in approaching God: that if we ask anything according to His will, He hears us. And if we know that He hears us—whatever we ask—we know that we have what we asked of Him" (1 John 5:14-15 NIV).

The key for us to be heard by God and see our prayers answered lies here - that we ask according to His will. How do we know God's will? We know His will and desires through the Bible, the Holy Spirit's guidance, prophecies, revelation, dreams, and visions, and sometimes through the counsel of our leadership to whom we submit.

We should be thankful that God does not accede to all our prayer requests. Only some things we ask for are good, beneficial, unbiased, and timely. God sets the rule clearly – He hears us when we ask according to His will. And He is a God who watches over His Word to perform it.[2] In other words, He is obligated to do what He says and will fulfill what He promises. He is faithful and true. He is a sovereign and all-knowing, wise God. He is our Father who loves us enough to say yes and, other times, no.

Being a mother, I understand this principle well. Despite my immense love for my children, I may not always agree with their wishes and demands. Some requests may be more appropriate for a different time, while others I may reject outright. Likewise, when we approach God with our requests, He will evaluate our intentions and desires. It is impossible for us to conceal anything from His Spirit.

There is a classic example in the Bible when God answered a man's request far beyond whatever he had asked. That man is King Solomon. In 1 Kings 3:11-13, God, in response to King Solomon's request, said to him: "Since you have asked for this and not for long life or wealth for yourself, nor have asked for the death of your enemies but for discernment in administering justice, I will do what you have asked. I will give you a wise and discerning heart, so that there will never have been anyone like you, nor will there ever be. Moreover, I will give you what you have not asked for—both wealth and honor—so that in your lifetime you will have no equal among kings."

It illustrated here that our requests could please God so much that He will give generously, not withholding any blessings from us, and answer us beyond our imagination and asking.[3] What a comfort this brings!

The Principle of Binding and Loosing

In Mathew 16:19, the Amplified Bible says, "I will give you the keys (authority) of the kingdom of heaven; and whatever you bind (forbid, declare to be improper and unlawful) on earth will have (already) been bound in heaven, and whatever you loose (permit, declare lawful) on earth will have (already) been loosed in heaven."

The spiritual principle of binding and loosing in prayer is powerful. Jesus freed many individuals from demon possession and sicknesses during His time on earth. In Mark 3:27, Jesus explains the significance of seizing the possessions of the strongman by first binding him. The strongman is referred to as Satan, and his possessions are what he controls or binds. In Mathew 12:22, Jesus delivered a demon-possessed man who was blind and mute by first binding the devil. Another instance was a woman crippled and bound by a spirit of sickness for eighteen years. She could not straighten up until Jesus healed and freed her from captivity.[4]

When we bind demons in Jesus' name, they are prohibited from operating and we can command them out. For example, we can pray this way: "I bind the spirit of confusion in his mind, and I command all lies, anxieties, and fear to leave in Jesus' name." In Greek, to "loose" means to get free, detach, and release from bonds, dissolve anything bound or destroy. So, in our prayer, we can loose someone from any demon spirit that is binding or holding them in bondage.

Let me sum up - We are operating in our Kingdom authority when we command diseases and demons to be bound, and loose people from their bondages (such as illnesses, depression, curses, witchcraft, perversion, fear, addiction, rejection, and shame) in Jesus' name.

Praying without Ceasing

Most of us know the Bible verse "Pray without ceasing" from 1 Thessalonians 5:17. Although praying is not a challenge to most of us, it can be difficult to maintain a consistent prayer routine. Nonetheless, it is important to keep praying even when it is difficult and not to lose heart. Perseverance is key to seeing prayers answered.

Today, we are living in a world of instant gratification. If we want to purchase a book or meals and have access to information, teachings, songs and music, movies, or any products and services, we can get immediate access with a click to order from our phones and computers right away. Everything is within a hand's reach. It is fast and convenient. Indeed, we must thank technological advancement and the brilliant minds behind these accessibilities and convenience. On the flip side, we may be accustomed to an expectation that the answers to our prayers ought to be as instant as we can get in the natural realm. In reality, God responds to our prayers in different ways and timing, which often differ from what we might expect.

Years back, when I worked for the church as a ministry staff, my income was not high, but it was sufficient to get by. I often prayed for financial provision, especially when I needed funds for overseas mission trips. One Sunday, a preacher came to speak at the church, whom I knew but was not close to. He did not know about my financial struggles. After his sermon, the preacher quickly left the aisle, but before he did, he put something in my hands. I was surprised that it was dollar notes (I cannot recall the exact amount now). It was unexpected and unusual for a preacher to give money to someone in my position, as it is more typical for us to support them financially. Nonetheless, I was extremely grateful for his kindness.

Besides discovering that God can provide for my needs in His way and time, my eyes were opened to see that in His sovereignty, God can choose to answer our prayers creatively. And this, indeed, was one unconventional way. The experience left me feeling humbled and encouraged by God's love.

P-U-S-H

Have you ever heard of the "P-U-S-H" corporate prayer initiative from years ago that was popular in the Church? It stands for "Pray Until Something Happens," and it demands faith, perseverance, and sheer tenacity on our part. In other words, we should keep going and keep praying until we see a breakthrough.

However, sometimes in life, the enemy tries to make us feel hopeless, doubt God's plan and promises, and give up before they are fulfilled. Waiting can be long and arduous, but we must resist the temptation to quit prematurely. We need to stay strong in faith because we only lose if we give up. Remember that Jesus already defeated the devil, so we are fighting from a position of victory. Rest assured that your victory is guaranteed.

As stated in Ephesians 6:18a from The Message Bible, prayer is a vital aspect of the ongoing spiritual battle. We are to pray hard and long. The Bible acknowledges that prayer is no easy task, so we must persist until we see favorable outcomes. It is important to remember that our prayers have a dynamic impact on the spiritual realm, even if we do not see immediate results. Please do not give up too soon, my friend.

Think of the unwavering perseverance of a pregnant mother who endures those grueling hours of labor until her baby is born. It requires intense effort and determination, but the overwhelming sense of relief and joy when she finally holds her precious newborn is the ultimate gift and reward. It is only a matter of time before the answers to your prayers become apparent. Some answers may come swiftly, while others might take longer. However, it is imperative to remember that a delay does not necessarily signify a denial from God. If you keep praying, you may eventually see the fruits of your labor. I want to remind you once again not to give up!

When you pray, you create a protective shield around yourself, your loved ones, communities, cities, and nations. Your generation is waiting to see the positive impact of your persistent prayers. During these uncertain times, it is important not to give up but instead intensify our prayers.

Are you ready to take your prayer life to the next level and experience God's blessings through effective prayers? Do not settle for less! Be brave and tenacious, and persistently pursue and hold onto God's promises until they are fulfilled. In essence, be a prayer warrior and fight the good fight!

---

[1] Mark 16:17-18
[2] Jeremiah 1:12
[3] Ephesians 3:20
[4] Luke 13:11-13

3

The Holy Spirit is Your Helper

"In the same way, the Spirit helps us in our weakness. We do not know what we ought to pray for, but the Spirit Himself intercedes for us through wordless groans. And He who searches our hearts knows the mind of the Spirit, because the Spirit intercedes for God's people in accordance with the will of God" (Romans 8:26-27 NIV).

As I mentioned earlier, prayer is not an effortless task. It requires hard work. However, there is good news - the Holy Spirit is always present to assist us in our prayers. He is our prayer companion, guiding us and instructing us on how to pray according to God's perfect will. Knowing that we are praying correctly, in accordance with God's truth and will, is an amazing feeling! We can be confident that God is more than willing to respond to our prayers.

Mathew 7:7-8 NASB says, "Ask, and it will be given to you; seek, and you will find; knock, and it will be opened to you. For everyone who asks receives, and the one who seeks finds, and to the one who knocks it will be opened." The remarkable truth is that God listens to our prayers and is always willing to answer them. We do not need to beg or plead with Him to listen to us. As Martin Luther aptly said: "Prayer is not overcoming God's reluctance but laying hold of His willingness."[1]

Praying in the Spirit

Many times, when I do not know what and how to pray about a matter or person, I would begin to pray in the Spirit. This is because I can trust the Holy Spirit to help me to pray for God's perfect will. When I pray in tongues, I allow the Holy Spirit to pray directly through me, allowing my emotions, prejudice, and opinions to get out of the way.

Praying in tongues is a precious and powerful gift accessible to all believers. It is also a sign of our authority in Christ, as mentioned in Mark 16:15-18 NKJV: "Go into all the world and preach the gospel to every creature. He who believes and is baptized will be saved; but he who does not believe will be condemned. And these signs will follow those who believe: In My name they will cast out demons; they will speak with new tongues; they will take up serpents; and if they drink anything deadly, it will by no means hurt them; they will lay hands on the sick, and they will recover."

Speaking in tongues is a form of communication with God, as stated in 1 Corinthians 14:2 NKJV. When we speak in tongues, we speak to God, not to men, and we speak myster-ies in the spirit. In verse 18, the apostle Paul highlighted that he spoke in tongues more than any other believer. Therefore, we should not underestimate or ignore this gift given to us by the indwelling Holy Spirit.

The apostle Paul further encouraged us to pray in the Spirit at all times and on every occasion.[2] This means that every moment is an opportune time to pray. You can pray in tongues while you shower, do the laundry, wash the dishes, drive your car, or walk your dog in the morning or night, and really, there is no fast rule about where and when to pray. The important thing is to learn to pay close attention and listen to the Holy Spirit. His voice may sound like a gentle whisper or a soft nudge or tug in your heart, an inner knowing or a thought in your mind. Recognizing His voice may require some practice, but it will be worth it.

Obey the Holy Spirit's Promptings

I remember feeling a sudden, intense desire to pray one morning. Without delay, I stopped my kitchen activities and proceeded to my room. Though unsure of what to pray specifically for, I heeded the prompting of the Holy Spirit. Suddenly, I found myself praying earnestly for my children. It almost felt like Hannah in the Bible, who had dedicated her child Samuel to God.[3] Here I was, consecrating my children to the Lord and for His Kingdom. I have always done that, but this time, it felt different. That experience left me feeling somewhat bewildered but spiritually fulfilling. It felt like a mission accomplished! The burden to pray, and specifically in this case, for my children, was lifted off me by the time I was done praying.

That day, I learned what yielding to the Holy Spirit in prayer looks like. Feeling the intensity of God's heart towards someone or something and praying in agreement with His Spirit is crucial. There may be times when you will feel a particular burden to pray for someone or some issues. When that happens, be obedient and willing to lay aside everything and start praying. If you do not know what to pray, you can pray the scriptures or in tongues. Remember, the Holy Spirit is your helper. Pray until you feel the burden or weight lifted off you. So, stay open to the Holy Spirit throughout the day, be alert in your spirit, and submit to His promptings. He is here to help us pray.

Prophetic Prayers

To pray prophetically means to pray with an understanding of God's heart and will through divine revelation. It is different from our usual intercession and supplication. You are still praying according to God's will, except now, you get first-hand information or insight from the Holy Spirit about a particular situation to pray effectively. And to put it candidly - it is like possessing spiritual intelligence, but I am specifically referring to the Holy Spirit.

The Holy Spirit may highlight a specific thing to you, such as the enemy's tactics, and expose his lies, deception, or occultic element so it can be dealt with. He may also lead you to speak God's blessings or prophesy over some areas of a person's life (whether it be the areas of finances, family, health, career, relationships, destiny, etc.).

Through prophetic insights, people would usually encounter the love of God during prayers. I remember a time when I prayed for a couple whom I hardly knew. It was our first conversation. While praying with them, the Holy Spirit showed me a vision of the husband as a young boy. This insight enabled me to pray more effectively for him despite not knowing them well. On another occasion, I was asked to pray for a young lady I had just met for the first time. I trusted the Holy Spirit to guide me and prayed specifically about her identity and relationship with the Lord. After the prophetic prayers, she felt reassured and loved by God, knowing that He alone understands the true condition of her heart. I observed a noticeable change in her facial expression as she exuded a sense of peace and joy.

Hearing what the Holy Spirit says as you undertake this exciting prayer strategy is essential. But how do we listen to what He is saying? How do we know if we get it right? Jesus says, "My sheep listen to My voice; I know them, and they follow Me" (John 10:27 NIV). In other words, it is an innate ability for every believer to hear God's voice. We all can hear His voice. It is never a matter of whether we can hear God speak, but rather how to recognize the ways He speaks.

We know from the Bible that God can speak in varied ways and choose to communicate in any way He likes. God is a creative communicator. He can speak to us through His written Word, angels, dreams, visions, and various other mediums such as music, art, movies, nature, circumstances, people, books, prophets, teachings, signs, and wonders. In

Numbers 22, God even opened a donkey's mouth to speak. This shows that He can use any means necessary to communicate with us.

God is constantly communicating with us, and we must learn to tune our spiritual senses to hear Him. This requires intentional effort and practice to develop our spiritual senses. Hebrews 5:14 says: "But solid food is for the mature, who because of practice have their senses trained to distinguish between good and evil." The translated Greek word for "train" is "gymnazo," which implies training and working out vigorously like an athlete in a gym. Likewise, we need to take our senses to God's gymnasium, train ourselves, and build our confidence to hear His voice for ourselves and others.

To become confident and competent in discerning God's voice, we must practice intentionally to receive revelations and release the prophetic word through our prayers. Do not be afraid to make some mistakes and learn from them. You will never learn until you are willing to step out of your comfort zone and allow yourself to be stretched.

Keep a Prayer Journal

Keeping a journal is an excellent way to develop your ability to hear God's voice and hone your spiritual senses. By recording your revelations and keeping track of their fulfillment, you can become more attuned to how God communicates with you. Whether you receive revelations through dreams, visions, songs, books, or a particular scripture that jumps out at you while reading the Bible, the key is to remain open to the Holy Spirit's leading every day.

There may be times when the Holy Spirit is trying to draw your attention to something specific, such as an incident or an unusual phenomenon in the sky. It is fascinating how many people have seen double rainbows and been encouraged by the signs in the sky. I once had an extraordinary experience when I saw small feathers three times in a single day. Despite being in different places each time, I could still see those feathers in my path no matter where I went. I knew that God was highlighting the presence of angels to me.

To start journaling, choose a method that works best for you. You can be creative and use your phone, or you can do an audio recording if you prefer. The essential thing is to remember that your prayer journal is a way of communicating with God and developing your spiritual senses to hear His voice. It is often easy to miss what God is communicating to us amid our busyness unless we intentionally capture and tune in to hear Him speak. Therefore, keeping a prayer journal to remember what God is saying and how He responds to our requests is important.

Keeping your journal simple and focused on recognizing how God communicates with you is key. You can record dates and specific prayer requests, so you can look back and see how God answered them. This will help build your faith gradually as you witness God's faithfulness and the powerful ways He answers your prayers. In the process, you will also draw closer to Him as you seek to hear His voice.

Your prayer journal can become a source of inspiration and a reminder of God's goodness during challenging times. So, write down what God is saying to you, including key scriptures, prophecies, or impressions that come to mind during your prayers. Even if you are unsure, write it down or record it on your phone. With practice, you will become more skilled at hearing God's voice. You can also use your journal to record your testimonies and give God praise for answered prayers.

In summary, prophetic prayer is a powerful tool for bringing forth God's plans and purposes on earth. It enables us to overcome demonic obstacles and propels us into the goodness of God. Prophetic prayers can bring healing, deliverance, restoration, victories, direction, reconciliation, provision, promotion, and breakthroughs. By keeping a journal, you can document these powerful transformative experiences, seal the memoirs of God's miracles, love, and blessings, and grow to recognize how God speaks.

---

[1]   deeperchristianquotes.com/prayer-is-laying-hold-of-gods-willingness-martin-luther/

[2]   Ephesians 6:18

[3]   1 Samuel 1:27-28

4

Decree and Declare

By definition, a decree is a legally enforced official order or decision. It is a royal command with kingly authority. As seen in the Book of Esther, the person who issues the decree must have the legal authority to do it. Once a decree is written and sealed by the king's signet ring, it carries the king's authority, and the decree cannot be revoked.[1] That means it cannot be withdrawn, reversed, or canceled.

We see the power of a decree in Esther 8. Mordecai wrote a decree in the king's name, and it empowered the Jews to overturn completely their enemies' plans. Instead of destruction, the Jews were able to defend and protect themselves. As a result, they experienced a great victory and celebration.

When we make a prophetic decree in Jesus' name, it is sanctioned by His divine authority and power. It speaks firmly of God's unchanging Word over our lives and situations, thwarts the enemy's plans, and leads to breakthroughs and miracles.

God's Will on Earth as it is in Heaven

Imagine how God's will get done on earth as it is in heaven when you release a decree. The spoken Word of God from our mouth creates and brings transformation to situations and people's lives. In Psalm 33:9, the Bible says, "For He spoke, and it came to be; He commanded, and it stood firm." Notice that God did not just think out loud or dream about good ideas in His mind. He spoke! God's Word is living and active.[2] It has life and creative power. God spoke, and the universe came into form and beauty, as we see in the book of Genesis.

God has shown us that our words have the power to create. However, it is not just any words or wishes – it is the living Word of God and decrees inspired by the Holy Spirit. When we speak with faith, our words can significantly impact both the natural and spiritual realms. And this can result in supernatural answers to our prayers.

God also promises in Isaiah 55:11 NASB: "So will My Word be which goes out of My mouth. It will not return to Me empty, without accomplishing what I desire, and without succeeding in the purpose for which I sent it." So, let me nail it down - You must send the Word. You are like God's agent or messenger, declaring on earth what He has spoken and established in heaven. Hence, the prophetic decree is a powerful and creative word. My friend, I strongly encourage you to lift your voice, speak out, and boldly declare God's Word.

Angelic Assistance

When we speak God's Word, it not only fulfills His purpose but also summons angels to provide assistance. Angels are not the cute cherubs with halos and wings, as commonly illustrated in books and cartoons. They are spiritual beings sent by God to serve His people.[3]

In the book of Daniel, God sent His angel Gabriel to provide prophetic insight and understanding to Daniel about future events immediately after his prayer. During the evening sacrifice, Gabriel appeared to Daniel and said, "Daniel, I have come here to give you insight and understanding. The moment you began praying, a command was given. And now I am here to tell you what it was, for you are very precious to God. Listen carefully so that you can understand the meaning of your vision" (Daniel 9:21-23 NLT).

Later, in chapter 10, Daniel prayed for understanding and humbled himself before God, and an angel visited him. The angel reassured Daniel, saying, "Don't be afraid, Daniel. Since the first day you began to pray for understanding and to humble yourself before your God, your request has been heard in heaven. I have come in answer to your prayer" (Daniel 10:12). Similarly, in the New Testament, we learn how an angel miraculously rescued Peter from prison after the church prayed earnestly.[4]

It is, therefore, imperative for us to understand that angels listen to, obey, and act upon God's Word. When we speak God's Word, we give voice to His commands, and angels are dispatched to carry out His divine purposes on earth. As Psalm 103:20 NLT states, "Praise the LORD, you angels, you mighty ones who carry out His plans, listening for each of His commands."

Declare it!

According to Webster's dictionary, "declare" means to make known formally, officially, or explicitly. When we decree and declare in prayer, we are partnering with the Holy Spirit to speak into existence for the will of God to be established. It is an official announcement for divine alignment to manifest in the natural realm.

Look at Job 22:28 in the Amplified Bible: "You will also decide and decree a thing, and it will be established for you and the light (of God's favor) will shine upon your ways." The New King James Version says, "You will also declare a thing, and it will be established for you; so light will shine on your ways."

When we pray, it is important to listen to the Holy Spirit and partner with Him to declare God's will. Many Christians have used the prayer of Jabez as a personal declaration for many years. This prayer is based on 1 Chronicles 4:10, where Jabez asked the God of Israel to bless him and expand his territory. He also asked God to keep him from harm and free from pain, and God granted his request. Another powerful declaration that we can pray is found in Luke 4:18-19. The New International Version states, "The Spirit of the Lord is on me because He has anointed me to proclaim good news to the poor. He has sent me to proclaim freedom for the prisoners and recovery of sight for the blind, to set the oppressed free, and to proclaim the year of the Lord's favor."

Some of the most uplifting scriptural declarations can also be found in Deuteronomy 28. For instance, verse 6 declares that we are blessed on both our coming in and going out. Furthermore, verse 13 in the New Living Translation states,

"The Lord will make you the head and not the tail, and you will always be on top and never at the bottom."

Isaiah 54:2 is personally one of my favorite prophetic declarations. The verse reads, "Enlarge the place of your tent, stretch your tent curtains wide, do not hold back; lengthen your cords, strengthen your stakes." With faith, we can boldly proclaim that God is fulfilling His promises and bringing an increase to our lives. The past hindrances will no longer hold us back, and we will make room for more and the new. We are expanding in all directions, and God's blessings shall overflow in our lives in Jesus' name!

These are some examples of prayer declarations based on scriptures that will encourage us and empower our prayer life, especially in challenging times. It is important to remember that every declaration we make must be based on God's infallible Word, His ways, and divine revelation.

In the upcoming chapter, we will dive into various decrees and declarations that pertain to different aspects of our lives. I highly recommend creating your own decrees that are customized to your specific situation. You can use the blank pages labeled "Write My Decrees" at the end of the book, to write down and declare God's promises and Word, which can unleash miracles and blessings. I am truly eager to hear your success stories of victories and breakthroughs!

---

[1] Esther 8:8

2 Hebrews 4:12

3 Hebrews 1:14

4 Acts 12:5-11

5

Effective Prayers

I want to suggest some areas where you can pray effectively using decrees and declarations. While not all-inclusive, these areas cover the essential aspects of our lives. Remember that these prophetic decrees serve as a guide, not a formula. Hence, you have the freedom to use your own words and expressions. It is crucial to understand that declaring God's Word is a potent tool for seeing His purpose, solutions, and interventions come to fruition for us, others, and nations.

While Jesus was on earth, He demonstrated the power of His Word by speaking and producing supernatural results. For instance, He calmed a storm by commanding the winds and seas to cease.[1] He also spoke to a fig tree, and it withered.[2] Furthermore, He healed the sick by sending His Word. In Luke 7, a Roman officer understood the power of Jesus' spoken word. His servant was sick and near death. While Jesus was on His way to the man's house to heal his servant, He was halted and asked to simply speak the word. Being a man of authority, the Roman officer knew there was power in the spoken word for something to be carried out effectively. Listen to what he says, "I am not even worthy to come and meet You. Just say the word from where You are, and my servant will be healed" (Luke 7:7 NLT). The servant had indeed been completely healed.

Let us look again at Isaiah 55:11 in the Amplified Bible: "So will My Word be which goes out of My mouth; it will not return to Me void (useless, without result), without accomplishing what I desire, and without succeeding in the matter for which I sent it." Put simply, when God's Word is delivered or sent, it will successfully achieve His intended desires and outcomes. The New Living Translation says, "It is the same with My Word. I send it out, and it always produces fruit. It will accomplish all I want it to, and it will prosper everywhere I send it." Yes, the declared Word of God from our mouths is always productive and fruitful.

So, start declaring with faith and authority what God says today. I trust you will witness God's results manifesting for you and others. Have faith and anticipate success and fruitfulness!

1. My Identity

It is important to understand that you are who God has declared you to be. You assume a new identity when you believe in Jesus and accept Him into your heart. Therefore, your past no longer has power over you and cannot restrict you. Your new identity is genuinely based on God's eternal, unchanging Word. So, go ahead and make these declarations boldly.

"As it is written in Your Word, I declare that…"

- *I am a new creation, and my citizenship is in Heaven. (2 Corinthians 5:17; Galatians 2:20; Philippians 3:20)*

- *I am a child of God, purchased by the blood of Jesus. (John 1:12; Romans 8:15-16; 1 Corinthians 7:23; Galatians 3:26; Ephesians 1:5)*

- *I am Christ's beloved. I am chosen and loved by Him. Nothing can separate me from His love. (John 15:19; Romans 8:35-39; 1 Peter 2:9)*

- *I am a crown of glory and a royal diadem in God's hand. (Isaiah 62:3)*

- *I am a friend of God, and He knows me. (John 15:13-15; James 2:23)*

- *I am set apart unto the Lord. I belong to Jesus. (1 Corinthians 6:20; 2 Timothy 2:21)*

- *I am created for God's glory. (Isaiah 43:7)*

- *I am never alone because Jesus is always with me, and He lives in me. (Deuteronomy 31:8; Psalm 27:10;*

94:14; John 14:20; Galatians 2:20; Hebrews 13:5b)

- *I am an heir of God and co-heir with Jesus. (Romans 8:17)*

- *I am saved by grace through faith in Jesus, not by my good works. (Ephesians 2:8-9)*

- *I am more than a conqueror through Christ Jesus. I am a winner, not a loser. (Romans 8:37)*

- *I am blessed and not cursed. God has blessed me with every spiritual blessing in the heavenly places with Jesus. (Ephesians 1:3)*

- *I can do everything through Christ who strengthens me. (Psalm 28:7-8; Philippians 4:13)*

- *I am strong in the Lord and the power of His might. (Ephesians 6:10)*

- *I am a co-laborer with the Holy Spirit. I partner with Him in everything I do and in great exploits for His Kingdom. (John 14:16; Acts 1:8; 1 Corinthians 3:9)*

- *I am creative and ingenious because God is. His Spirit lives in me daily. (Genesis 1:27; Exodus 31:1-6)*

- *I am God's Masterpiece. I am unique, precious, and fearfully, and wonderfully made by God's own hands.*

He fashioned me in His very image. (Psalm 139:14; Ephesians 2:10)

2. My Calling and Purpose

One common question many young people and children get is, "What do you want to be or do when you grow up?" That question rarely fails to put some fear and stress on many. The good news is that God already knows, even if we do not have a clue. I believe that our ultimate calling and purpose in life is to represent Jesus and express Him in our generation, regardless of our chosen path.

The apostle Paul emphasizes in Ephesians 1:4 that God has chosen us to be holy and blameless in His sight, even before the foundation of the world. Similarly, in Romans 8:29, he highlights that those whom God foreknew have been predestined to be conformed into the likeness of His Son, Jesus Christ.

In his book, *Your Highest Calling*, Bill Hamon, the founder of Christian International Ministries, also shares that God's highest calling for our lives is to be ultimately conformed to Jesus' likeness.

"I decree that every demonic assignment sent to distract, hinder and derail me from God's calling shall be abolished in Jesus' name. I declare..."

- *God's plans are to prosper and not to harm me. He is giving me hope and a future. (Jeremiah 29:11)*

- *God is directing and establishing my footsteps every day. (Psalm 37:23; Proverbs 16:9; 20:24)*

- *God is working all things together for my good. (Romans 8:28)*

- *God has begun a good work in me and will complete it until the day Jesus appears. (Philippians 1:6)*

- *I can trust God to open the right doors for me and shut those not deemed fit. (Revelation 3:7)*

- *I have a God-given destiny, and I will fulfill it. All the days ordained for my life were planned and written in His book in Heaven. (Jeremiah 1:5; Psalm 139:16; Romans 8:29; Ephesians 2:10)*

- *I will delight myself in the Lord, and He will give me the desires of His heart. (Psalm 37:4)*

- *I will be transformed into the image of Jesus my Lord with ever-increasing glory every day. (Romans 8:29; 2 Corinthians 3:18)*

- *I will do the good works God has prepared in advance for me to do. (Ephesians 2:10)*

- *I am empowered supernaturally by the Holy Spirit to be Jesus' witness wherever I go. (Acts 1:8)*

- *I will trust God from the bottom of all my heart. I will listen to His voice in everything I do, and He will show me which way to go. (Proverbs 3:5-6)*

- *I declare that God's purpose for my life shall prevail. (Proverbs 19:21)*

- *I will live a life worthy of the Lord and please Him in every way. I will bear fruit in every good work and grow in the knowledge of God. (Colossians 1:10)*

- *As God's faithful steward, I will use His gifts to me to serve others according to His grace. I will serve with the strength God provides so that He alone may be praised and glorified in all things. (1 Peter 4:10-12)*

- *I choose to forget those things which are behind and reach forward to those things which are ahead. Therefore, I will press toward the goal for the prize of the upward call of God in Jesus. (Philippians 3:13-14)*

3. **My Health and Healing**

Our health and well-being matter to God. He wants us to be in good health and strength all our days. Not just physically but also emotionally, spiritually, and relationally.

I like how the Amplified Bible has revealed the secret to health in Proverbs 3:7-8: "Do not be wise in your own eyes; fear the Lord (with reverent awe and obedience) and turn (entirely) away from evil. It will be health to your body (your marrow, your nerves, your sinews, your muscles—all your inner parts) and refreshment (physical well-being) to your bones." Did you get that? The key is to trust the Lord fully, fear God, and shun evil.

"I decree that as my days are, so shall my strength be. My health will prosper even as my soul does. I declare..."

- *My body is a temple of the Holy Spirit. Therefore, sicknesses and diseases cannot remain in my body. I command every pain and sickness to leave in Jesus' name! (Isaiah 58:8; Jeremiah 17:14; 1 Corinthians 6:19)*

- *He is the God who heals me and binds up my wounds. (Exodus 15:26; Jeremiah 30:17; Psalm 30:2; 103:3; 147:3)*

- *I declare, by Jesus' stripes, I am healed! (Isaiah 53: 4-5; 1 Peter 2:24)*

- *I will be in good health as my soul prospers spiritually.*

(3 John 1:2)

- *The joy of the Lord shall be my strength. (Nehemiah 8:10)*

- *God's Word is life to me. It brings health and healing to my body. (Proverbs 4:20-22)*

- *I will not fear and be dismayed, for He is my God. He will strengthen, help, and uphold me with His righteous right hand. (Isaiah 41:10)*

- *I will live and not die and declare the works of the Lord. (Psalm 107:20; 118:17)*

- *I will live a long full life for God's glory. (Psalm 91:14-16)*

- *I remain confident of this: I will see the goodness of the Lord in the land of the living. (Psalm 27:13)*

- *As for me who fear God's name, the Sun of Righteousness will rise with healing in His wings, and I will go free, leaping with joy like calves let out to pasture. (Malachi 4:2)*

- *In Christ, I live and move and have my being. Therefore, I have full access to His divine nature and godly virtues. (Acts 17:28; 1 Corinthians 13:4-7; 2 Corinthians*

13:5; Galatians 5:22; Colossians 1:27; 2 Peter 1:4)

- In peace, I will lie and sleep, for the Lord makes me dwell in safety. (Psalm 4:8)

- I will not be afraid when I lie down. My sleep will be sweet. (Proverbs 3:24)

- The Lord gives sleep to me, His beloved. (Psalm 127:2)

- The Lord gives strength to me and blesses me with His peace. (Psalm 29:11)

- I am casting all my cares on Jesus, for I know He cares for me. (1 Peter 5:7)

- The Lord is my keeper and my shade at my right hand. The sun will not strike me by day nor the moon by night. The Lord will keep me from all evil and preserve my life. (Psalm 121:5-7)

- I command all fear, anxieties, and tension to leave me in Jesus' name. The Lord will keep me in perfect peace, for I trust Him and choose to fix my thoughts on Him. (Isaiah 26:3; John 14:27; 2 Thessalonians 3:16)

- I have the mind of Christ, and I choose to fix my thoughts on what is true, honorable, right, pure, lovely, and admirable. I will think about things that are excellent and worthy of praise. (1 Corinthians

2:16; Philippians 4:8)

- *I have not been given a spirit of fear but of power, love, and a sound mind. (2 Timothy 1:7)*

4. My Family and Friends

All our relationships are fundamentally built upon God's principle of love. Building a family and maintaining healthy relationships with friends, colleagues, and the Christian community takes love. One practical and powerful way of loving our family and others is through fervent prayers. Setting aside time to pray for our loved ones every day is essential. Our prayers are building a hedge of divine protection over them.

"As it is written in Your Word, I declare that..."

- *As for me and my house, we will serve the Lord. (Joshua 24:15b)*

- *As a family, we shall always be harmonious, sympathetic, loving, compassionate, and humble. (1 Peter 3:8)*

- *I will obey my parents in the Lord and honor them. This pleases God, and I will live long on the land the Lord is giving me. (Exodus 20:12; Deuteronomy 5:16;*

Ephesians 6:1-2; Colossians 3:20)

- *My family and I are devoted to one another in love. We shall honor one another above ourselves. (Romans 12:10)*

- *We will be diligent in keeping the unity of the Spirit through the bond of peace. (Ephesians 4:3)*

- *We will love the Lord our God with all our heart and with all our soul and with all our mind and with all our strength. (Mark 12:30)*

- *The angel of the Lord encamps around my family, who fears God, and he rescues us. (Psalm 34:7)*

- *I bind the work of the enemy who has blinded the minds of my unbelieving family members/friends (their specific names) from the gospel of Jesus. I command every deception and antichrist spirit to loose them and shall not operate in their minds anymore in Jesus' name. I declare that they will know the truth and be set free. They will see the light of the glory of Jesus. I decree that God's will for them to be saved shall prevail. They will call on Jesus' name and be saved. (John 3:16; 8:32; Acts 16:31; Romans 10:13; 2 Corinthians 4:4; 1 Timothy 2:4; 2 Peter 3:9)*

- *I will be quick to listen and slow to speak. (James 1:19)*

- *God's favor surrounds me and my family like a shield. (Psalm 5:12)*

5.   My Finances

"Seek the Kingdom of God above all else, and live righteously, and He will give you everything you need." (Mathew 6:33 NLT)

The Kingdom works this way: Put God first, and the increase will follow. Remember, He promises to give you everything you need, not everything you want. There is a difference.

"I am blessed to be a blessing. I decree that God has given me the power to make wealth and the wisdom to steward it for His Kingdom. I thank God that His blessings shall overtake me, and He will not withhold any good thing from me. I declare..."

- *My God will liberally supply; fill until full, my every need according to His riches in glory in Christ Jesus. (Philippians 4:19)*

- *God will bless my generosity, for I give to the poor. (Proverbs 22:9)*

- *The blessing of the Lord makes me rich, and He adds*

no sorrow to it. (Proverbs 10:22)

- *I bring my tithes to God's house faithfully. I thank God that He will open the windows of Heaven and pour out abundant blessings that there will not be enough room to store them. (Malachi 3:10)*

- *I am a cheerful giver. I will reap bountifully as I sow bountifully. (2 Corinthians 9:6-7)*

- *I will seek the kingdom of God first and His righteousness, and all these things shall be added to me. (Mathew 6:33)*

- *When I give, I will receive in full - pressed down, shaken together to make room for more, running over, and poured into my lap. (Luke 6:38)*

- *I will honor God with everything I own; give Him the first and the best. Therefore, my barns and vats will be filled with plenty and bursting over. (Proverbs 3:9-10)*

- *The Lord is my Shepherd, and I lack nothing. (Psalm 23:1)*

6. My Education and Career

"Work willingly at whatever you do, as though you

were working for the Lord rather than for people. Remember that the Lord will give you an inheritance as your reward, and that the Master you are serving is Christ." (Colossians 3:23-24 NLT)

"As it is written in Your Word, I declare that..."

- *My God is able to make all grace abound to me so that having all sufficiency in all things at all times, I may abound in every good work. (2 Corinthians 9:8)*

- *I will not be anxious about anything. By prayer and supplication, with thanksgiving, I will make all my requests to God. His peace which surpasses all understanding will guard my heart and mind. (Philippians 4:6-7; 2 Thessalonians 3:16)*

- *I command all fear and anxieties to leave in Jesus' name. God is with me, and I will not be afraid or discouraged. He will strengthen me and help me. He will hold me up with His victorious right hand. (Isaiah 41:10)*

- *I cast all my cares on the Lord, and He will sustain me. He will never let the righteous be shaken. (Psalm 55:22)*

- *I declare my help comes from the Lord, the Maker of heaven and earth. Nothing is impossible with God.*

(Psalm 121:2; Luke 1:37)

- *I will seek God's will in all I do, and He will show me which path to take. (Psalm 25:4; 27:11a; Proverbs 3:6)*

- *God resists the proud but gives grace to the humble. Therefore, as I humble myself, He will guide me in what is right and teach me His way. (Psalm 25:9; James 4:6)*

- *I have the wisdom of God, for He has given generously to me without reproach when I asked. (James 1:5)*

- *I am the head, not the tail; above and not beneath. I choose to stay obedient to God's commandments in every circumstance. (Deuteronomy 28:13)*

- *I am the salt and light of the world. My light will shine before people so that they will see my good works and glorify my Father in heaven. (Mathew 5:13-16)*

7. **My Safety and Protection**

"Based on Psalm 91, I declare..."

I dwell in the shelter of the Most High, and I will rest in the shadow of the Almighty.

I will say of You, my Lord, "You are my refuge and fortress, my God, whom I trust."

Surely You will save me from the fowler's snare and the deadly pestilence.

You will cover me with Your feathers, and under Your wings shall I find refuge. Your faithfulness will be my shield and rampart.

I will not fear the terror of night, nor the arrow that flies by day, nor the pestilence that stalks in the darkness, nor the plague that destroys at midday.

A thousand may fall at my side, ten thousand at my right hand, but it will not come near me. I will only observe with my eyes and see the punishment of the wicked.

I declare, "The Lord is my refuge," and I make the Most High my dwelling. Therefore, no harm will overtake me, and no disaster will come near my tent.

You will command Your angels concerning me to guard me in all my ways. They will lift me up in their hands so that I will not strike my foot against a stone.

I will tread on the lion and the cobra. Yes, I will trample the great lion and the serpent.

Because I love You, therefore You will rescue me. You will protect me, for I acknowledge Your name.

I will call on You, and You will answer me. You will be with me in trouble. You will deliver me and honor me.

You will satisfy me with a long life and show me Your salvation.

8.   **The Nations**

"To get nations back on their feet, we must first get down on our knees."- Billy Graham[3.]

"I urge, then, first of all, that petitions, prayers, intercession and thanksgiving be made for all people - for kings and all those in authority, that we may live peaceful and quiet lives in all godliness and holiness. This is good, and pleases God our Savior" (1 Timothy 2:1-3 NIV). The Message Bible says, "Pray especially for rulers and their governments to rule well so we can be quietly about our business of living simply, in humble contemplation. This is the way our Savior God wants us to live."

When a nation faces any form of upheaval, the people will suffer its consequences, and it becomes difficult to live peacefully, let alone preach the gospel and advance the Kingdom. Therefore, we must pray fervently for all those in authority in our nations. Lift them by names before the throne of God if you can.

The Bible states that when wicked people are in power, the people groan.[4] We all desire to experience joy and peace rather than misery and chaos. Therefore, there is a great need for godly leaders to govern and establish laws that adhere to God's principles and values in all nations.

"I declare over my nation/another country..."

- *"Arise, shine (name of country), for your light has come, and the glory of the Lord rises upon you. See, darkness covers the earth and thick darkness is over the peoples, but the Lord rises upon you and His glory appears over you. Nations will come to your light, and kings to the brightness of your dawn."* (Isaiah 60:1-3)

- *I declare that dominion belongs to the Lord, who rules over the nations. (Psalm 22:28)*

- *Father, I thank You that when we, Your people who are called by Your name, humble ourselves, pray and seek Your face and turn from our wicked ways, You will hear us from heaven, forgive our sin, and heal our land. (2 Chronicles 7:14)*

- *I declare that God is the refuge and strength of my nation, an ever-present help in trouble. When we pass through the deep waters, God is with us. When we pass through the rivers of difficulty, they will not sweep over us. We will not be burned when we walk through the fire of oppression. The flames will not consume us! (Psalm 46:1; Isaiah 43:2)*

- *I decree that God will place the right people in the appropriate roles and positions at the perfect time within our government. God changes times and seasons. He removes kings and raises kings. (Daniel 2:21)*

- *I decree that every wicked plan and purpose in and against my nation shall be thwarted. I declare the plans of the Lord shall stand firm and His purposes through all generations in Jesus' name. (Psalm 33:10-11)*

- *I decree that the godly in my nation shall be placed in authority and power. Our people will rejoice again! (Proverbs 29:2)*

- *I decree my nation shall be blessed and prosperous because God is the Lord and has chosen us for His inheritance. (Psalm 33:12)*

- *Father, I declare Your kingdom has come, and Your will be established in all nations. (Mathew 6:10)*

- *Father, I declare all the praise belongs to You alone. Be merciful and bless our nation and people everywhere. Make Your face smile with favor on us. Your ways and Your saving power shall be known throughout the earth. I declare the nations shall praise You, and the whole world will sing for joy because You govern the nations with justice. You will guide us and bless us richly. The earth will yield its harvest, and all nations will fear You and praise Your Holy Name. (Psalm 67)*

---

[1] Mark 4:39
[2] Mark 11:12-14; 11:20
[3] justdisciple.com/missionaries-quotes-on-prayer/
[4] Proverbs 29:2

Dear Father, I thank You for giving me the privilege and access to come before Your throne of grace boldly every day. Today, I ask that You reignite my passion for prayer and take me deeper into the chambers of Your heart. Help me to feel Your love towards others whenever I pray. I want to pray effectively so that I can see tangible results in my life and the lives of those around me. Above all, I yearn to experience the joy of knowing You more and spending time in Your presence.

Holy Spirit, I invite You to teach me to hear Your voice with greater clarity so I may partner with You to establish God's will on earth. I am excited about this new adventure of faith with You!

Thank You, Father, for the assurance that You hear my prayers when I pray according to Your will. I know that You care deeply about every detail of my life and others. May my life be a living testimony to the power of prayer and the love of Jesus.

Amen.

Conclusion

Prayer is not a mundane spiritual practice but an anointed weapon for spiritual warfare. It is also a lifelong privilege that allows us to connect with God personally. Through prayer, we enter the presence of the Almighty God, who listens to our deepest desires. As Jeremiah 29:12 ESV says, "Then you will call upon Me and come and pray to Me, and I will hear you." When we pray, angels are dispatched to carry out God's plans for our lives and the world. We become actively engaged in advancing God's Kingdom.

The most important thing is that God takes pleasure in our prayers and our presence. By praying, we demonstrate our dependence and faith in Him, no matter how we feel inside. It is essential to remember that God receives our prayers, and we should not let the devil's lies and guilt prevent us from praying.

Dear friend, I want to encourage you that your prayers are incredibly important and valuable. I recently had a conversation with my son, who was feeling frustrated about unanswered prayers. However, I encouraged him to keep praying and trust that God always listens, even if we do not see immediate results. Every prayer counts and makes a difference. Through prayer, we can unleash God's power, resulting in miraculous occurrences in the physical realm. Prayer should always be our first resort, not our last. Prayer can change situations and human hearts, but we must trust God to answer in His way and time.

Finally, living in purity and holiness is crucial for effective prayer. According to the Bible, our sins can hinder our prayers, and God will not hear us.[1] However, Jesus demonstrated deep reverence towards the Father, resulting in God always hearing His prayers.[2] Proverbs 15:8 NIV emphasizes that God detests the sacrifice of the wicked but finds delight in the prayers of the righteous. The English Standard Version puts it simply, "The prayer of the upright is acceptable to Him." This verse underscores that living a holy and righteous life is the key to being heard by God. Additionally, James 5:16b reminds us that the prayer of a righteous person is powerful and effective.

Oswald Chambers once said, "Prayer does not fit us for the greater work; prayer is the greater work."[3] Therefore, do not allow the devil to discourage or distract you from praying. Instead, continue to pray passionately and sow every seed of faith behind your prayers, trusting that God will bring breakthroughs for His glory. Your efforts are never in vain, and God rewards what you do in secret when you pray. Persevere and trust God for supernatural results; before you know it, your next breakthrough is here. So, keep the faith!

---

[1] Psalm 66:18; Isaiah 59:2

[2] John 11:42; Hebrews 5:7

[3] utmost.org/classic/greater-works-classic/

Write My Decrees

Write My Decrees

Write My Decrees

Write My Decrees

Glory is a self-taught artist and prophetic voice from Singapore. Her journey with Jesus began at the age of nine and has since grown into a deep and special relationship. Since her youth, she has served the Lord in various roles and ministries including worship, prayer, missions, and prophetic presbytery. Her passion lies in prayer, revival, creativity, the prophetic, and the supernatural.

In 2012, Glory completed her Apostolic Prophetic training with the Christian International Global Network. Most recently, in 2022, she and her husband, Joseph, graduated from the School of Apostles and Prophets by RIG Nation. Although she has never considered herself a writer, Glory penned her first book, *Praying with Power,* in response to her prophecies.

This practical guide is aimed primarily at teenagers and young adults, also known as "Gen Z," to inspire and empower them to pray confidently and fervently, experiencing God's blessings. However, individuals of all ages looking to elevate their prayer life can benefit from this insightful book.

To connect with Glory:

Facebook.com/HisGloryCarrier
www.glorypropheticart.com/books

www.ingramcontent.com/pod-product-compliance
Lightning Source LLC
Chambersburg PA
CBHW071233130726
47998CB00003B/938